SEDITION

David Wiltse

BROADWAY PLAY PUBLISHING INC
224 E 62nd St, NY, NY 10065
www.broadwayplaypub.com
info@broadwayplaypub.com

SEDITION
© Copyright 2008 by David Wiltse

First printing: April 2008
I S B N: 0-88145-381-1

Book design: Marie Donovan
Word processing: Microsoft Word
Typographic controls: Ventura Publisher
Typeface: Palatino
Printed and bound in the U S A

ORIGINAL PRODUCTION

SEDITION was first produced at the Westport Country Playhouse (Tazewell Thompson, Artistic Director; Jodi Schoenbrun-Carter, Managing Director) in Westport CT on 4 August 2007. The cast and creative contributors were:

SCHRAG ....Chris Sarandon
CASSIDY .... Mark Shanahan
TELLIG ....Bryant Martin
HARRIET .... Hanna Cabell
CHANCELLOR .... Colin McPhillamy
MEGRIM .... Jeffrey DeMunn

Director .... Tazewell Thompson
Set design ....Donald Eastman
Costume design ....Ilona Somogyi
Lighting design .... Robert Wierzel
Sound design .... Fabian Obispo
Stage manager .... Katherine Lee Boyer

CHARACTERS & SETTING

ANDREW SCHRAG, *late thirties to fifty, intellectual, proud*
HARRIET SCHRAG, *his wife, late twenties, smart, lively*
CASSIDY, *thirties, charming, weak*
CHANCELLOR, *forty-five to sixty-five, a politician at heart*
MEGRIM, *thirty to fifty, clever, pleasant, mean-spirited*
TELLIG, *college age male, naive, enthusiastic*

N B: The name Schrag rhymes with Prague.

Time: 1917-1918

The sets and props can be as minimal as possible. The object is to flow freely from one scene to the next with the aid of lighting to connote the end of one scene and beginning of another.

Place: Lincoln, Nebraska

in memory of my grandfather,
Andrew Schrag

and with gratitude to my brother, John Christopher
Wiltse, for his invaluable research

ACT ONE

Scene One

(A professor's office at the University of Nebraska.)

(ANDREW SCHRAG is seated as CASSIDY enters. They are friends as well as colleagues and at ease with one another.)

CASSIDY: *(Mock formality)* Herr Professor Schrag. *Wie geht's?*

SCHRAG: *Monsieur* Cassidy. *Comment ca va?*

CASSIDY: Lord, what a day! Spring has sprung, Andrew, "and all the drear hibernal clouds are now o'ershot with Phoebus' fulsome shards of gold."

SCHRAG: Heaven help me, the whimsy is upon him...What devilment are you up to now?

CASSIDY: Just avoiding my students... How are you, my friend? How is your very young and lovely lady bride? How is marriage treating you after six months?

SCHRAG: I tell you, Cassidy, taking a modern woman as a wife is like coming out of a dark cave into a hall of light and mirrors. I never knew I was such a mess until my wife pointed it out.

CASSIDY: It sounds unpleasant.

SCHRAG: On the contrary. It's bracing. I am still the topic of discussion, after all. *(Laughs)* That's a joke I couldn't have made about myself before Harriet enlightened me.

CASSIDY: My knowledge of women is broad,
but shallow...

SCHRAG: So one hears.

CASSIDY: ...but I believe the husband is supposed
to be in charge.

SCHRAG: As the bull is in charge of the matador.
Women have ways of winning far beyond our
understanding, my friend.... Perhaps it's witchcraft.

CASSIDY: You seem to take it well.

SCHRAG: I've never been more constrained, nor happier.
Odd, isn't it? ...What brings you to my office, other
than flight from your students?

CASSIDY: I come to beg a boon. A small boon. A
boonette, as we ought to say in French, but don't.

(There is a knock on the door.)

SCHRAG: *(German—pronounced hair eye-n) Herein.*

*(Enter TELLIG. He is a first-year student in German and is
filled with both the naivete and enthusiasm of youth.)*

TELLIG: Herr Professor Schrag?

SCHRAG: *Guten tag.*

TELLIG: Uh, um, *entschuldigen Sie, bitte. Darf ich Sie
steuren? (Sie steuren is pronounced zee shtoy-ren.)*

SCHRAG: You want to steer me?

TELLIG: Is that what I said?

SCHRAG: Did you mean to say *"stören"* instead of
steuren? (Stören is pronounced, roughly, shtirren.)

TELLIG: My accent is so bad. Maybe I should have
come in with my hands in the air. *"Nicht scheissen,
nicht scheissen." (Scheissen is pronounced sch-eye-zen.)*

SCHRAG: You have just commanded me not to shit.

TELLIG: Oh, my God, no.

(CASSIDY *laughs.*)

SCHRAG: I can accommodate you for the moment, but I can't comply forever.

(*Pause.* TELLIG *is confounded.* CASSIDY *is chuckling to himself, trying not to intrude.*)

SCHRAG: I'm joking...I think you meant *schiessen...* (*Schiessen is pronounced sch-ee-zen.*) What can I do for you, Mister Tellig...perhaps in English?

TELLIG: You know who I am?

SCHRAG: Well, I know you tend to chew on your pencil, you have trouble with vocabulary and declensions, and I know you sit in the third row by the window, and you often find something outside much more interesting than your humble professor.

TELLIG: No, no, I...

SCHRAG: If I ever found all of my students paying attention I would think I'd sprouted another head on my shoulder.

TELLIG: I'm sorry...

SCHRAG: But you're not afraid to try which takes courage and I admire the effort... Now, how can I help you?

TELLIG: I'm leaving school and I need permission to drop my courses, otherwise I'll get Fs and it will be hard for me to get back in when I come back.

SCHRAG: I'm sorry to hear you're leaving the university. Why is that?

TELLIG: (*Proudly*) I'm going over. As soon as I can.

SCHRAG: Over?

TELLIG: To the war. To Germany.

SCHRAG: The war's in France and Belgium,
not in Germany.

TELLIG: Well, to fight the Hun.

SCHRAG: The Hun.

TELLIG: The Boche...the Germans. The ones we're
fighting.

SCHRAG: But Mister Tellig, this country isn't at war.

TELLIG: But we will be soon, won't we? I mean, I know
President Wilson spoke to the Congress and said we
had to and I guess he would know...

SCHRAG: Do you know why Doctor Wilson thinks
we have to go to war?

TELLIG: Well...things are just intolerable, he says.
We can't let them talk to us that way.

SCHRAG: Have the Germans been talking to you,
personally, Mister Tellig?

TELLIG: I know you're joking again but the Germans
said they were going to submarine any ships they want
to.

SCHRAG: Any ships approaching British ports, I believe.
The British have offered to do the same.

TELLIG: Yes, but not with submarines.

SCHRAG: The difference?

TELLIG: Well, submarines, I mean, you can't see them,
can you? That's not the way to do things.

SCHRAG: There've been fifteen attacks on American
merchant ships approaching British ports since the
fighting began two years ago. Do you know how many
Americans have died?

TELLIG: Not really. Quite a lot.

SCHRAG: Three.

TELLIG: I didn't know that. I thought it was...well,
I didn't know that.

SCHRAG: I'm afraid there are quite a number of things
we should know that we don't. You're not alone in this.

TELLIG: Well, still...President Wilson says we have to
make the world safe for democracy and I think that's
important.

SCHRAG: The British have been in India for more
than two hundred years and haven't made India a
democracy. France hasn't freed Algeria...Mister Tellig,
the King and the Kaiser decided to have a pointless
war and now our envious president, feeling ignored,
wants to join in. I'm afraid I don't see how democracy
is involved in this insanity.

TELLIG: Um...I didn't pay that much attention to what
he said; the president was pretty sure about it, though.

SCHRAG: How old are you, Mister Tellig?

TELLIG: Nineteen.

SCHRAG: Nineteen. I'm more than twice your age.
Will you let me guide you and see if we can reason
our way through this problem together?

TELLIG: Like Socrates.

SCHRAG: The old gentleman just rolled in his grave, but,
yes, alright, in the Socratic manner, if you will... Let me
offer you a hypothetical situation and see if it clarifies
things for us...If I presented you with a gun and told
you that you could make the world safe for democracy
if you blew your brains out, would you do it?

TELLIG: (Pause) Well, but that's not really the way it
works, is it?

SCHRAG: No, not really. I would have to give you a uniform first, then ask you to blow your brains out for democracy.

TELLIG: No, but you can't be sure that's going to do it... I mean, just because you say it will.

SCHRAG: But if President Wilson says it will, you are willing?

TELLIG: I want to do my part, everybody does.... Actually I'd like to get behind one of those machine guns. They say that German Maxim gun is the best but I'll bet the British Lewis gun is pretty swell, too.
They can go four hundred and fifty rounds per minute, isn't that something? Did you know they can even shoot a machine gun in the airplanes now? Right through the propeller! Can you believe it? It's a thing called an interrupter; it works off a cam on the propeller shaft. This German fellow Fokker, who makes all those planes, came up with it. Well, the Germans are good at that sort of thing.

SCHRAG: Anthony Fokker is a Dutchman.

TELLIG: And he's making airplanes for the Germans?

SCHRAG: He's making them for the money. Hiram Maxim, who invented the German machine gun that you so admire, is an American. There are many fortunes to be made in a war. But we seem to have wandered a bit from the Socratic method. Let me offer you another hypothetical situation.

TELLIG: Shoot. (Laughs) Well, you know what I mean.

SCHRAG: If I could give you the machine gun of your choice and produce a young German of your age and put him here before you and suggest that you blow his brains out to make the world safe for Doctor Wilson's version of political organization, would you do it?

TELLIG: I just want to do my duty. No one asks you to shoot a fellow in cold blood.

SCHRAG: I believe that's precisely what they'll ask you to do. Four hundred and fifty times a minute if you're lucky enough to get a machine gun.

TELLIG: We can't let the Germans tell us what to do, though.

SCHRAG: Actually, I think they are telling us what not to do in order to avoid casualties.

TELLIG: Same difference. It's a matter of honor, isn't it?

SCHRAG: There were eight hundred thousand casualties on both sides in the battle of the Somme. Did you know that, Mister Tellig? It's a blood bath.

TELLIG: And that's what we're going over there to stop. If the Europeans can't do it, we will.

SCHRAG: The Europeans are experts at it. They've been slaughtering each other for centuries. Do you think Americans have anything to teach them in that department?

TELLIG: With all due respect, Professor, I think Americans can pretty much teach anybody anything there is. And I'm not the only one who thinks so.

SCHRAG: Why not let them fight it out as they've always done? Does it matter who wins? When Wilson was elected he said we must remain neutral.
   When he was re-elected, his slogan was, "He kept us out of the war." Three months later he's decided we must swim in European blood. Are you sure you really want to follow the man in the top hat just because he thinks he knows better about how to live your life than you do? Mister Tellig, judging by your name, you're German, not English. We've fought two wars with the British, none with the Germans.

TELLIG: Professor, I'm an American. That's it.
My country, right or wrong.

SCHRAG: The rest of that phrase is: if right, to be
kept right and if wrong, to be set right.

TELLIG: It's no good, Professor, because I got a
preference for America and that's how it's going
to stay. If we're going over, I'm going, too.

SCHRAG: *(Resignedly)* Yes, of course... You have my
permission to drop the course.

TELLIG: Thank you, sir. And thanks for helping me to
think about all this. *Auf wiedersehen. (Nods to* CASSIDY*)*
Professor Cassidy.

CASSIDY: Good luck, Mister Tellig.

SCHRAG: Goodbye, Mister Tellig.

*(*TELLIG *exits.)*

CASSIDY: Blood-thirsty young man, isn't he?

SCHRAG: He repeats what he's heard, that's all...
I didn't handle it well, did I?

CASSIDY: Nonsense. You couldn't have stopped him.

SCHRAG: He came in here for advice. He likened me to
Socrates, of all things. And I failed him.

CASSIDY: His mind was made up.

SCHRAG: We have to get them to think! That's our job,
we're educators, we are supposed to guide them, teach
them!

CASSIDY: There are other ways. This is what I came to
see you about. You're sincere in your opposition to the
war, aren't you?

SCHRAG: Do you think I was lying to the boy?

CASSIDY: If you knew how to lie you'd probably
be running the whole university instead of just the
German department.

SCHRAG: That's very cynical. Is that a French affectation?

CASSIDY: Have you thought about actually doing
something to keep us out of the war?

SCHRAG: What can I do? I fear Wilson has his heart set
on it.

CASSIDY: You could speak out publicly. We're having a
rally in a few days. I'd like you to join us and say a few
words.

SCHRAG: What sort of rally?

CASSIDY: We want to let the government know that we
don't want to go to war.

SCHRAG: And who is this "we"?

CASSIDY: I'm one of the organizers, along with some
other members of the faculty.

SCHRAG: I didn't know you were politically minded,
Cassidy.

CASSIDY: *(Brogue)* Ah, sure, it's part of me Irish heritage,
don't ya know? *(Regular voice)* We Irish aren't great
friends of the British, as you may have heard.

SCHRAG: And you want me to speak to a group of...
what? ...Agitators, troublemakers, immigrants? No, no.

CASSIDY: It won't be a rabble. Mostly students. Just
think of all those empty heads ready to be filled with
the first persuasive voice they hear. You can be their
received wisdom on the subject.

SCHRAG: I don't know if you're being serious or not, but
it's a responsibility. Some of them are still little sponges.

CASSIDY: I'm very serious. That's why I'm asking you to join us. I can't think of anyone I'd rather have telling them what to think.

SCHRAG: Not what to think. Just to think for themselves.

CASSIDY: None better. You're very eloquent.

SCHRAG: You're not going to flatter me into it, Cassidy.

CASSIDY: Speaking the truth isn't flattery.

SCHRAG: *(Amused)* And still you persist... No, politics is all a bit too greasy for my taste. I tend to gag.

CASSIDY: You don't have all those facts at your fingertips because you're not interested.

SCHRAG: I can watch two dogs fighting without wanting to join in.

CASSIDY: Even if one of them is your dog? We're all politicians now, like it or not.... We need your wisdom, Andrew. Socrates did not hesitate to speak out when his wisdom was needed.

SCHRAG: Socrates was put to death by the Athens city council for being a nuisance and a nag...

CASSIDY: Well, it's fortunate then that this is not Athens. A man can say what he wants without having hemlock thrust upon him.

SCHRAG: I'm really not the man for this sort of thing, despite my close kinship with Socrates.

CASSIDY: Who is? Who else will do it?

SCHRAG: Sorry, Cassidy.

CASSIDY: Will you sign our petition, at least? It's just a statement urging the government to remain neutral as we have been for the past two years. It would mean a great deal to have your name on our list. You are well-known and respected.

SCHRAG: All the more reason I'd rather not be involved. A man in my position has to be very careful what he lends his name to. Say what you like, you know that most people crying against our entering the war have a certain—taint—to their credentials.

CASSIDY: Will you think about it, at least?

SCHRAG: Ah, well, ask me to think and you've found my weak spot. I'll think—but I don't think I'll act.

(Lights down on SCHRAG office.)

(Lights up on SCHRAG home.)

(As the lights change, we hear the sound of war pandemonium, cheers, martial music, then a radio announcement that war has been declared.)

Scene Two

(The SCHRAG home)

(A few weeks after the first scene)

(HARRIET, SCHRAG's wife, is there when SCHRAG enters. HARRIET is a good deal younger than SCHRAG.)

HARRIET: Oh, Andrew, I'm so glad you're home. Guess what happened, you'll never guess, it's so exciting.

SCHRAG: *(Charmed)* I love your enthusiasm. I walk into the house and here you are, bouncing with energy...

HARRIET: You make me sound like a puppy. This is exciting.

SCHRAG: What is it? What wonderful thing has happened?

HARRIET: Now don't indulge me, share with me... Mrs Webster had the baby! Isn't it wonderful?

SCHRAG: That is wonderful. Are they both healthy?

HARRIET: Yes, yes, even though the baby was nine pounds. Can you imagine, a woman that small?

SCHRAG: Ouch.

HARRIET: Let's go see them now. I've been waiting and waiting all day but I wanted us to go over together.... I thought you'd be here an hour ago. Why are you so late?

(Deliberative pause from SCHRAG, *which* HARRIET *picks up on.)*

SCHRAG: *(Somberly)* I passed Meisner's delicatessen on 14th Street on my walk home. It's just been burned by a mob of "patriots".

HARRIET: Good heavens. Why?

SCHRAG: It seems they were incensed because the poor man hadn't changed the name of sauerkraut to "liberty cabbage".

HARRIET: You're joking.

SCHRAG: Some of them were throwing stones at his dachshund...for being a "German" dog.

HARRIET: Oh, Andrew, that can't be, no one would do that.

SCHRAG: They were doing it.

HARRIET: You didn't get involved, did you?

SCHRAG: I suggested that they stop. They suggested that I go elsewhere... *(Self contempt)* Sorry to say, I took their advice, although I did give them a very disapproving look.

HARRIET: Well, what were you supposed to do against a bunch of hooligans?

SCHRAG: "Supposed to do" by whose standards?
...A man was lynched in Cincinnati yesterday for
opposing the war.

HARRIET: No!

SCHRAG: It's called "patriotism". The last refuge of
a scoundrel, according to Samuel Johnson.
The Chancellor of Syracuse University has told his
students that it is "religious" to hate the Germans.
Apparently, the good Lord would approve.

HARRIET: ...This is frightening.

SCHRAG: I'm sorry. I should have realized it would
upset you...

HARRIET: I don't need to be protected, I'm not a child...
but what does all this mean for us? Will you be a target?

SCHRAG: Why would I?

HARRIET: You're head of the German department.
That makes you at least as much an enemy as a poor
little dachshund, doesn't it?

SCHRAG: I'm not sure I like the comparison, but, unlike
the dog, I can do something to stop it...I'm thinking
of speaking at one of Cassidy's rallies.

HARRIET: No, Andrew.

SCHRAG: Just a few words.

HARRIET: Oh, I wish you wouldn't. You already told
him you wouldn't, didn't you?

SCHRAG: (Lightly) Consistency is the hob-goblin of little
minds.

HARRIET: No one is accusing you of having a little
mind...it would be very foolish to speak out publicly.

SCHRAG: (Mildly offended) Foolish? Foolish.

HARRIET: Now, Andrew, don't climb on your high horse, you're just talking to me.

SCHRAG: Do I have a high horse?

HARRIET: You do get a bit self-righteous at times, my dear, you'll admit that.

(SCHRAG *takes a very deep breath, exhales slowly.*)

SCHRAG: Did I marry a woman who is too perceptive?

HARRIET: No, fortunately, you married me.

(*They exchange an affectionate touch.*)

HARRIET: I don't know how Cassidy finagled you into speaking, but I really wish you wouldn't. I don't trust him.

SCHRAG: What do you have against poor Cassidy? I find him amusing.

HARRIET: I think he would flatter a toad if it suited his purpose. But it's not about Cassidy. We have friends, neighbors. We're at war, you might alienate some of them, you might turn them against us. You see the houses all around us displaying their American flags.
    They think of themselves as patriotic; how will they like it if you speak at a rally and call them scoundrels?

SCHRAG: Harriet, the country has gone berserk and the government is egging them on. Wilson wants hysteria. Someone has to speak out with a voice of reason.

HARRIET: Not you, it doesn't have to be you.

SCHRAG: Surely no one will be offended if I just offer my opinion.

HARRIET: You're not that naive, and yours isn't just any opinion...You are a very prominent man at a very vulnerable time...

SCHRAG: (*Admiring, amused*) You're so young. How can you be so certain of what's right to do?

HARRIET: (*Teasing*) Even without your great experience I know enough to run out of a burning building, not into it...I wish you wouldn't do this. Please.

SCHRAG: (*Resignedly*) All right. I won't wrestle with you all day over it. I won't speak at the rally.

HARRIET: Thank you. You know, that's one of the things I love best about you.

SCHRAG: Your ability to bend me to your will?

HARRIET: You're a rational man. You'll always do the right thing.

SCHRAG: Are they the same?

HARRIET: Come on, let's go see Mrs Webster and the baby...Do you realize you haven't even asked if it's a girl or a boy?

SCHRAG: I felt certain it was a girl or a boy. Was I wrong?...What is it?

(HARRIET *takes* SCHRAG's *hand*.)

HARRIET: Now you'll have to wait and see. Come, come with me, I can't wait any longer.

SCHRAG: I won't be expected to hold it, will I? ...I'm a little frightened by babies.

(HARRIET *kisses* SCHRAG.)

HARRIET: You are very brave to admit that. Would you have said that before me?

SCHRAG: I wouldn't have been looking at babies before you.

(HARRIET *leads him off and they exit. Lights down on* SCHRAG *home..Lights up on* CHANCELLOR AVERY's *office*.)

Scene Three

(A few weeks later)

(CHANCELLOR's office)

(A desk and a few chairs are all that are required in a minimal staging. This office can be a simple rearrangement of SCHRAG's office.)

(CHANCELLOR and MEGRIM. CHANCELLOR is a chemist who has advanced to the height of university politics, but he is still a bit stiff and awkward in the job. It is a skill learned through ambition, not a natural talent. MEGRIM is a very pleasant man. Even during the most serious questioning, his manner is disarmingly pleasant.)

CHANCELLOR: He'll be with us momentarily.

MEGRIM: And how are things with you, Chancellor? Is your contract going well?

CHANCELLOR: My contract?

MEGRIM: With the government? For research?

CHANCELLOR: *(A bit discomfited)* I wasn't aware...um...You are well-informed.

MEGRIM: Oh, I'm stoked to bursting with information. *(Laughs)* Touch me and I'll explode like a over-stuffed tick.... No, actually, the Defense Council does a good deal of research and pumps it into me.... But you're pleased with your arrangement for your work on— mustard gas, is it? ...Why do they call it mustard? Forgive my ignorance.

CHANCELLOR: In its impure form it smells a bit like mustard, or garlic. Some say horseradish. The pure form is odorless, of course. Undetectable. That's what we're striving for.

MEGRIM: Fascinating. I really wish I knew more about chemistry. Yours is certainly a valuable contribution to the war effort. And you're pleased with your arrangement?

CHANCELLOR: Oh, absolutely. I feel I'm doing important work and um...

MEGRIM: The army certainly agrees. And your remuneration is sufficient?

CHANCELLOR: Oh, indeed, very generous.

MEGRIM: Excellent. I'm very pleased, very pleased. I'll pass that on. There's no reason you shouldn't continue to have a mutually beneficial relationship.

(*Knock on door*)

CHANCELLOR: Come.

(CASSIDY *enters.*)

CHANCELLOR: Ah, Cassidy. Allow me to introduce Mister Megrim.

MEGRIM: Professor Cassidy, how good of you to come.

CHANCELLOR: Technically, Mister Cassidy is not yet a professor...

CASSIDY: Just an associate professor. A lowly grind, I'm afraid.

MEGRIM: Really? I wasn't aware. Well, I'm sure it's just a matter of time, eh, Chancellor?

CHANCELLOR: Well, um...

MEGRIM: (*To* CASSIDY) A word in the ear, here and there, can do no harm. (*Chuckles*) It's certainly a pleasure to meet you. I've heard so much about you.

CASSIDY: Really?

MEGRIM: All good, all good. (*Chuckles*)

CASSIDY: In that case, the pleasure's all mine.

MEGRIM: *(Abruptly but lightly)* Well, there's always someone.

CASSIDY: How do you mean?

(CASSIDY turns to CHANCELLOR for explanation.)

CHANCELLOR: Mister Megrim is with the state Council of Defense. The university encourages you to give him your cooperation. Strongly encourages you.

MEGRIM: I'm doing a little informal questioning— just chatting with some of the faculty. I find it most enjoyable talking with highly educated people like yourself. I learn so much about life from your enlightened points of view. *(Chuckles)* It's like going to college...You teach French, I understand.

CASSIDY: I try.

MEGRIM: French is such a beautiful language, isn't it?

CASSIDY: Yes, yes it is.

MEGRIM: Don't speak it myself. You're not a Frenchman, though, are you, Mister Cassidy?

CASSIDY: Oh, no, no.

MEGRIM: What is the affinity you have for the French?

CASSIDY: Well, they assisted us in a few revolutions against the British tyranny. We have a long memory.

MEGRIM: Us? You mean America?

CASSIDY: I was referring to the Irish, actually.

MEGRIM: Oh, you're Irish, are you, Mister Cassidy?

CASSIDY: *(Brogue, lightly)* Well, now how would ya be after meaning dat, Mister Megrim?

MEGRIM: *(Chuckling)* I think you know how I mean it.

CASSIDY: My father was from Dingle, County Kerry. My mother was from Omaha. What kind of Irish does that make me, then?

MEGRIM: *(Lightly)* The kind some people would call a Mick, although I wouldn't use a term like that myself.

CASSIDY: I'm pleased to hear of your restraint. *(To* CHANCELLOR*)* What is this all about? What is the Defense Council exactly?

MEGRIM: We're helping the federal government and the state militia to investigate questions of loyalty.

CASSIDY: Loyalty? To the university?

MEGRIM: To the nation. To the people. To our commitment to the war effort.

CASSIDY: You're questioning my loyalty?

MEGRIM: Oh, not at all, Mister Cassidy. You are loyal, aren't you?

CASSIDY: Certainly.

MEGRIM: That's what I assumed. It would be a sad state of affairs if those most privileged should hold our values less dear than the average man, don't you agree? ...But I'm told you had a few unkind words to say against our allies, the British, at some sort of mob assembly. *(Brogue)* Did you imagine yourself back in the auld sod there, trottin' the bogs, yellin' out any scurrilous ting you wanted about our ally in the war? *(Regular voice)* You're dancing a fine line, Mister Cassidy, careful you don't fall... Although, I know you Irish are light of foot.

CASSIDY: I'm American, too....

MEGRIM: Not first and foremost?

CASSIDY: ...and, as far as I know, I've got a perfect right to say whatever I want about the British or anyone else.

MEGRIM: Are you sure of your facts, there, Professor? Are you familiar with the Espionage Act passed in June?

CASSIDY: No.

MEGRIM: It makes it illegal to sully or impede the war effort or the government.

CASSIDY: Sully the... You mean we can't criticize the war?

MEGRIM: Or the government.

CHANCELLOR: The Board of Regents has decided that any teacher whose behavior is, uh, um, negative or halting, rather than aggressively in support of the government, shall be dismissed. Mister Megrim is helping with our inquiries to—uh—uncover um...

CASSIDY: It can't be against the law to criticize the government. That's outrageous.

MEGRIM: Is it? You would know best, I suppose, but Congress seems to like the idea. We are at war. Our nation is threatened. The times require unity of purpose, I'm sure you'll agree.

CASSIDY: I don't agree at all.

MEGRIM: Well, that's disappointing. I was hoping for your cooperation.

CASSIDY: What do you want me to do? Stand and cheer?

MEGRIM: I was hoping you could provide me with a list of names.

CASSIDY: Whose names?

MEGRIM: Of your speakers at your last anti- war rally.

CASSIDY: I don't recall.

(MEGRIM *ostentatiously consults the "files" on his lap.*)

MEGRIM: Well, there's always someone who remembers things of interest. We'll find them to help your memory.

CASSIDY: I'm not responsible for what others say, you know.

MEGRIM: If you'll indulge me one moment more... *(Reads from file)* "Any person with knowledge of the acts mentioned who conceals such information will be deemed to be an accessory..." Espionage Act.

CASSIDY: So it's not only illegal to criticize the war or the government, but even to hear such criticism. Does this mean we're supposed to spy on each other?

MEGRIM: It means we're all supposed to do our best to help in this time of crisis. Now, mind you, right at the moment we're not questioning your loyalty, Irishness not withstanding.
   But there is talk of some of your colleagues on the faculty—that their patriotism is not full- bodied.

CASSIDY: *(Amused)* Not full-bodied patriotism. I'm very surprised.

MEGRIM: You seem to find that humorous. Have I made a joke?

CASSIDY: It seems a light-hearted phrase.

MEGRIM: You take a number of things lightly, Professor, and you're not always as discreet as you might be, isn't that right, Chancellor?

CHANCELLOR: There are always, um...

MEGRIM: Yes?

CHANCELLOR: There are always a few disgruntled students. One doesn't pay too much attention to them. Female students sometimes misinterpret. We don't want the girls running the university, do we?

MEGRIM: *(Laughs)* What a thought. Like monkeys running the zoo... *(To* CASSIDY*)* Well, accusations, insinuations, you see how it is. *(He writes in file.)*

CASSIDY: I can't be expected...Women sometimes have hysterical reactions...

MEGRIM: They're not always as light- hearted as you, are they, Professor? Associate Professor... You taught at Hastings Normal College before coming to the university, I seem to remember.

CASSIDY: Yes. *(Pause)* Was there something...I thought I received an enthusiastic endorsement from Hastings.

*(*MEGRIM *looks at the file on his lap.)*

MEGRIM: Yes, well, officially.

CASSIDY: See here, Hastings was...I'm not going to stand here and deal with every innuendo...Spite, much of it was...I thought you wanted to talk about loyalty.

MEGRIM: A man's values are often linked. Have you observed that in your work with young people, Professor Cassidy? Deviation in one area leads to deviation in others. An unwholesome man has an accumulation of traits, not just one, that sets him apart from the honest man. A man who is not respectful of women—your flirt, for instance—is usually also disrespectful of serious men, of serious enterprise, even of God himself. Have you found that to be so, Mister Cassidy? Please tell me if I'm wrong...

CASSIDY: I'm sure I don't know.

MEGRIM: Really? I thought you might have some experience with issues of this sort. An unwholesome man drags his reputation behind him like a sack of stones.

He can't hide it, he can't get away from it, and, eventually, it will sink him.... Don't you think?

CASSIDY: I do see your point, Mister Megrim.

MEGRIM: Oh, good. Sometimes I'm just not very good
at explaining things. Makes me feel rather dense.

CASSIDY: That's not the word I would choose....
How may I help you with your inquiries?

MEGRIM: What I'd like from you, Mister Cassidy—
if you choose to cooperate...

CASSIDY: Of course.

MEGRIM: Lovely. I'd like to know who shares these
negative sentiments about the war and the government.
We have the names on your petitions. We know your
speakers. What we'd like to know are the names of
those who haven't signed on formally. We can only
watch those we know we should be watching. You
understand. *(Long pause)* Shall I rephrase it?

CASSIDY: ...You want to know who speaks against you,
who listens to them, and even those who might think
against you. I believe that's clear enough.

MEGRIM: Oh, excellent. It's always so much simpler
dealing with educated men.... Shall we begin?
(He prepares to take notes.)

*(Lights dim to denote brief passage of time. CASSIDY exits.
Lights up. Scene is the same.)*

MEGRIM: Charming man, isn't he? So much to hide, and
yet so talkative once he understood the situation.

CHANCELLOR: I must say, it was fascinating how you
went about it. I would have thought more directly,
you might...

MEGRIM: Would you confront a fat man by asking him
to admit he's obese? He would deny it and say he's
big-boned. A man's defenses are like a knotted ball of

twine, Chancellor. You must pick, and pick carefully, and, eventually, it will all unravel.

CHANCELLOR: Alexander solved the puzzle of the Gordian Knot by hacking it in two with his sword.

MEGRIM: Alexander was not seeking cooperation. The best time to get into a group is before their guard is up, not after. I think Mister Cassidy will be happy to serve from within.

CHANCELLOR: Do you think they're a group?

MEGRIM: Dissidence loves company, Chancellor. You can't conspire all by yourself.

CHANCELLOR: I find this very distasteful. Do you have what you need?

MEGRIM: The Defense Council will present you with a list of the suspects on your faculty. It will be up to the university to deal with them.

CHANCELLOR: We will certainly reprimand them severely...

MEGRIM: Are you mocking me? Do you imagine we've gone to all this trouble for a reprimand? These people must be publicly tried and dismissed. We would be hypocrites otherwise... The people cry out for action.

CHANCELLOR: Good Lord, man, you'll gut my teaching staff. You can't have them all.

MEGRIM: *(Pause)* We don't need them all; just enough to make the point. *(Smile)* We can winnow them out together. *(He starts to exit, pauses.)* I don't enjoy it either, you know. No one wants to watch educated men squirm. They have a higher calling, after all.

(Lights down on CHANCELLOR's *office.)*

(Lights up on SCHRAG *home.)*

Scene Four

(The SCHRAG *home.* HARRIET, SCHRAG, CASSIDY*)*

HARRIET: *(Irate)* You gave them his name?

SCHRAG: Harriet...

HARRIET: How could you do that?

CASSIDY: I had no choice.

HARRIET: You had the choice not to!

CASSIDY: I gave him the names of most of the faculty. I would have given him the Chancellor's name if he hadn't been sitting there. You don't understand the pressure I was under.

HARRIET: No, I don't.

CASSIDY: It was clear I would lose my position if I didn't cooperate.

HARRIET: And now others will, because of you.

CASSIDY: *(Brogue)* Ah, Harriet, pretty lass, don't be so angry with me...

HARRIET: I'm not a "lass". I'm a married woman, and I'd thank you to remember that.

CASSIDY: I meant no harm... *(To* SCHRAG*)* I meant no disrespect. I would never...

SCHRAG: We know that. He charms by habit, Harriet.

HARRIET: I don't find it as beguiling as you think, Mister Cassidy.

CASSIDY: I'm so sorry.

SCHRAG: Let's look at this calmly. I'm sure Cassidy didn't mean me any harm.

CASSIDY: Never, Andrew, never. If you do nothing, nothing will happen. You're already a cautious man, just stay cautious. Keep your head down and everything will be fine. This will blow right over.

SCHRAG: I don't intend to walk through life with my head down, but I'm doing nothing to trouble Mister Wilson. What can I do? What can anyone do?

CASSIDY: That's the safest attitude.

SCHRAG: *(Slightly offended)* I don't do it for safety. I would oppose him if I saw the point.... Wilson has his war. There's nothing I can do about it now.

CASSIDY: Quite right, that's exactly the attitude to take and we'll all get through this....

SCHRAG: What about you? Will you continue with your rallies?

CASSIDY: Oh, Lord no. I'm a lover, not a fighter.

HARRIET: *(Contemptuously)* Indeed.

CASSIDY: I must go.... Mrs Schrag, I'm sorry to have aggrieved you so.

HARRIET: *(Coolly)* Good night, Mister Cassidy.

CASSIDY: Good night, Andrew.

SCHRAG: Good night, Cassidy. And thank you for telling me.

(CASSIDY exits.)

HARRIET: Such a coward.

SCHRAG: Ah, Harriet, a little charity for poor Cassidy.

HARRIET: *(Contemptuously)* "A lover, not a fighter."

SCHRAG: He was frightened. He thought he was in danger.

HARRIET: A danger of his own making.

SCHRAG: You are a terror on the poor man. Put anybody's head in a vise and who knows how brave he'll be? I don't know how I'd do if the pressure were too high.

HARRIET: Couldn't you have been angry with him, at least?

SCHRAG: I hardly needed to since you were doing it for me.

HARRIET: I'm as aggrieved as you are.

SCHRAG: More so, it would seem. Allow me to have my own emotions, Harriet. You disgrace me by acting that way in front of a colleague.

HARRIET: *(Stunned)* By defending you?

SCHRAG: I'm not defenseless. Cassidy wasn't attacking me. All he did was tell the truth. I am opposed to them.

HARRIET: He sold you!

SCHRAG: You know Cassidy, he embellishes things. No one can harm me because of my thoughts.

HARRIET: How can you be so complacent? Don't you see the danger here?

SCHRAG: *(Lightly)* Well, I have you to protect me, my love.

HARRIET: Don't jolly me. Why do you men think we'll be content with a few pretty words?

SCHRAG: I've never seen this side of you, Harriet. There's a fierceness I don't recognize.

HARRIET: We're being threatened.

SCHRAG: Oh, I'm not in any grave danger...

HARRIET: We, Andrew. Don't imagine this affects only you. We're in this, and everything else, together.

SCHRAG: Yes, of course... *(Pause)* Do you think of me as an especially cautious man?

HARRIET: I would hope so.

SCHRAG: Cassidy kept saying that as if I... Is that the way you think of me?

HARRIET: I think of you as a highly sensible man. I count on it.

SCHRAG: Ah...

HARRIET: After all, you are the man of the family, as you point out.

SCHRAG: Now, my darling, I meant no offense by that.

HARRIET: Just a mild corrective.

SCHRAG: I've apologized. Peace. I'll keep my head down and my mouth shut—for both of us.

HARRIET: Thank you. You see, you are sensible.

SCHRAG: I'm a man in love and love conquers all— even the cautious.

(Lights down on SCHRAG *home.)*

(Lights up on CHANCELLOR's *office.)*

Scene Five

*(*CHANCELLOR's *office)*

*(*CHANCELLOR *is present.* SCHRAG *enters.)*

SCHRAG: You wish to see me, Chancellor?

CHANCELLOR: Ah, Professor Schrag. Good of you to come.

SCHRAG: Not at all. How can I help you?

CHANCELLOR: I have a bit of bad news, I'm afraid. We've just lost a student; one of yours, actually.

SCHRAG: How do you mean, one of mine?

CHANCELLOR: A boy named Tellig, was it? I think that's the name.

SCHRAG: *(Stunned)* Tellig.

CHANCELLOR: You know him?

SCHRAG: Yes, I know him, of course I know him. What happened?

CHANCELLOR: Killed in France. Terrible loss to all of us, of course.... Don't believe I knew him myself...

SCHRAG: *(Very shaken)* He's been killed?

CHANCELLOR: Well, yes, as stated.

SCHRAG: He was a boy, just a boy!

CHANCELLOR: Terrible thing of course, but he died for his country.

SCHRAG: He died for Wilson's fantasy. What could be more ludicrous?

CHANCELLOR: Get hold of yourself, Schrag.

SCHRAG: I could have stopped him.

CHANCELLOR: This kind of talk is dangerous.

SCHRAG: How much more dangerous not to have done anything?

CHANCELLOR: Be careful, Professor. You must have heard about the Defense Council; this odious man, Megrim... You're too important to this institution for me to lose you over an excess of sentiment. Mourn the boy but be circumspect about it, have some sense of proportion... Was he a particularly brilliant student? I don't understand the, uh, intensity of your...

SCHRAG: Sometimes it's the student we can not reach who affects us most. Sometimes it's the lost sheep.

CHANCELLOR: Very biblical, I'm sure.... I didn't realize you were such a romantic, Schrag. It's not your fault, not your responsibility. No one's to blame...

SCHRAG: No one's to blame? Was he struck by lightning? He died because of messianic lunacy and a vast national effort at stupidity.

CHANCELLOR: Good lord, man, keep this folly to yourself, others can hear you. I'm not sure I'm not obliged to report you myself.... If I'd known it would bring on a case of the wobblies, I wouldn't have told you. I had no idea you were so emotional. I've always regarded you as a rational man.

SCHRAG: My response to insanity is entirely rational— albeit inadequate.

CHANCELLOR: *(Pause)* Yes, well, calm yourself. You'd be advised to keep your response *in camera*, as it were... Now, I suppose we'll need to have a ceremony at the University chapel, since he's the first to die in this glorious cause.

SCHRAG: I think I should speak at the ceremony.

CHANCELLOR: Given your current frame of mind, I think it would be very unwise.

SCHRAG: I think I must. I owe him that much.

CHANCELLOR: He won't know, Schrag. The boy is dead.

SCHRAG: I will know.

CHANCELLOR: There's no advantage to wallowing in it. Let us do the expected thing and have it done with.... You will speak appropriately, I trust.

SCHRAG: Entirely appropriately.

(Lights down on SCHRAG's *office.*

(Lights up on SCHRAG *home.)*

Scene Six

(The SCHRAG *home.* HARRIET, SCHRAG*)*

HARRIET: Did you know the boy? You never spoke of him.

SCHRAG: He was a mediocre student. There was nothing to set him apart in the classroom.

HARRIET: Then why must you speak at the ceremony?

SCHRAG: I had a moment with him, a chance to dissuade him.... If I had been more persuasive, if I had tried harder, he might not have gone to war.

HARRIET: You had a moment with him? But Andrew, surely those who rush to enlist have a lifetime of reasons.

SCHRAG: And a torrent of encouragement from that high-minded moralist in Washington.

HARRIET: You always speak of him—not the policy, not the government—as if it were a contest between you and Wilson.

SCHRAG: Whom else should I blame?

HARRIET: Conditions, economics, history, Congress, the whole force of European politics...

SCHRAG: We must all take responsibility for our actions—or inactions. And so must he.

HARRIET: Andrew, sometimes you seem furious that your will is being denied, that someone else will have his way. Why do you take it so personally?

SCHRAG: Ideas are personal, Harriet. Beliefs are personal. They affect the way we live our lives and the way we think about ourselves. Wilson's ideas and beliefs are causing our young men to die. Stupidity at the top is an insult to all of us who think. If no one else holds him responsible, I do.

HARRIET: Forgive me for saying so, my dear, but this screams of vanity on your part. Your thoughts are not equal to his. He's the leader of the nation. Don't go to that podium because of your own self-regard.

SCHRAG: *(Pause; carefully)* Harriet, it seems to me that you have become increasingly critical of me of late. I have indulged this because it seemed to give you pleasure.

HARRIET: I thought you understood that...

SCHRAG: Please don't interrupt. I have taken what amusement I could find in this, but it now seems to me that it's not an exercise in self-examination, as you would have it, but genuine disapproval. One in which you take some delight.

HARRIET: I'm trying to protect you. I don't want you to say anything—careless—about Wilson in a public forum. Cassidy has warned us.

SCHRAG: Cassidy exaggerates.

HARRIET: I live in this community, Andrew, not in an ivory tower at the university.
   We have friends, neighbors...you will alienate them, you will turn them against us, and I will be tarred by the same brush. People will think I'm also a German sympathizer.

SCHRAG: *(Shocked)* Is that how you think of me, a German sympathizer? Both sides are lunatic; I want us to remain neutral.

HARRIET: Don't tell me that part of your defense of Germany doesn't come from your parents.

SCHRAG: *(Pause)* I forgot that your people were English.

HARRIET: I feel a kinship with England now. Don't ask me to be rational about it.

SCHRAG: But, I do. I ask everyone to be rational.

HARRIET: They're at war, Andrew. We can't just ignore our emotions. It's not human.

SCHRAG: You have no family involved. I have no family involved.

HARRIET: That doesn't matter. The English are my people, they're part of who I am. You feel the same way, I know you do, no matter how much you try to be above all that. No one can help it.

SCHRAG: Good God, are you and I at war with each other now? Has it come to that?

HARRIET: *(Pause)* Andrew, don't go to the ceremony.

SCHRAG: Of course I'll go. I have to go.

HARRIET: Don't speak, then, if you're going to do it in this vein. Please, darling. For me.

SCHRAG: *(Pause)* You make great demands.

HARRIET: Do not put us in harm's way...please... for my sake, if not your own.

SCHRAG: The boy is dead, Harriet.

HARRIET: And there's nothing you can do about it now. Why risk our place in the community, if you can't change things?

SCHRAG: But there are others I might influence. I have to try, don't I?

HARRIET: No! Why must you make the heroic gesture? I want to raise a family here. I'm not with you in this, Andrew. You're doing it alone but it will hurt both of us. Is that what you want?

(SCHRAG *looks at* HARRIET *for a long time, struggling with himself.*)

SCHRAG: Would you have me fail the boy twice?

HARRIET: I expect you not to fail me.

(SCHRAG *exits.*)

(Lights down on SCHRAG *home.)*

(Lights up on chapel.)

Scene Seven

(The ceremony)

(The University Chapel. A podium will serve as the set. CHANCELLOR *is at the podium, preparing to speak.* SCHRAG, HARRIET, *and* CASSIDY *enter and stand a distance from the podium.* MEGRIM *stands nearby.)*

(We hear the final notes of funereal music.)

CHANCELLOR: *(To congregation)* This is a sad day for all of us gathered here. It is a sad day for the University to have lost a young man of such outstanding promise.... But, in a larger sense, it is a proud day, too. It is a day in which we can say that we have given the finest of our youth in defense of our noble cause. We, too, by his sacrifice, have shown our willingness to carry the banner of freedom in the face of furious assault by an implacable enemy. Herman Tellig—loving son, devoted Christian, ardent student, friend to all who knew him—has given the last full measure of devotion, as Lincoln said, for the security of our great people, the freedom of our homeland, the sanctity of our ideals... Sadly, he will not be the last of our youth to fall in defense of democracy, but they will not die in vain. The noble cause for which they struggle will prevail, America will prevail, truth and honor and freedom will

always prevail, thanks to the devotion and courage
of young men like Herman Tellig...God bless Herman
Tellig, our first to fall.

(CHANCELLOR *steps away from the podium and joins*
MEGRIM. SCHRAG *makes a move towards the podium.)*

SCHRAG: Chancellor...

(HARRIET *holds* SCHRAG's *sleeve.)*

HARRIET: *(Hushed)* Andrew, please...be careful.

SCHRAG: I weary of that.

CASSIDY: Let it go, Andrew. It's not worth it.

SCHRAG: If it isn't, nothing is. *(He looks to* CHANCELLOR
for permission. To CHANCELLOR*)* A few words only.

(CHANCELLOR *looks uncertainly towards* MEGRIM *who
signals his approval.)*

CHANCELLOR: *(Hushed; to* SCHRAG*)* Appropriately, man.

SCHRAG: *(To congregation)* This boy was my student.
We have been told repeatedly that he has not died in
vain.... I don't know what that can possibly mean....
It is said that our children will ask us what we did in
this bloody war. 'Til now, I can only answer that I
wavered. I saw the idea of war brewing in the mind
of Wilson and his cadre of bankers and Wall Streeters
and I was annoyed, but did nothing. I saw the lust
for war come to a blaze and I was alarmed, but
did nothing. I saw us plunged pointlessly into the
European conflict, booted in like the town simpleton
lured to the edge of a ditch, and still I did nothing,
said nothing. I waited for someone else to stand
athwart the path of lunacy and stop it.

I waited for someone else to descry the obvious
nudity of our would-be emperor. But no one did, and
who was I to withstand the storm? I could say it was
wrong, but they could say it was patriotic. That's no

contest to a nation in a feverish mind.... So, how shall
I answer Herman Tellig when he asks what I did in this
insanely bloody conflict in which America has no part?
This war, in which our security is not threatened?
This war so devoutly wished by a man who thinks
himself messiah, bringing transformation at the point
of a sword? What could I do to stop Herman Tellig
from dying in this war? I could have taken to the streets
when others did. I could have cried out about the
madness until the heavens rang...I should have stopped
him if I had to wrestle him to the ground. But I did
nothing. Smug in my disapproval, I did nothing...
Now, I can only ask his forgiveness. God bless you,
Herman Tellig, our first martyr to the presidential ego,
our first sacrifice on the altar of international finance.

MEGRIM: Put him on the list. That is sedition.

(Black out)

END OF ACT ONE

ACT TWO

Scene Eight

(*Lights up on* SCHRAG *home.*)

(HARRIET *is alone, briefly.* CASSIDY *enters.*)

CASSIDY: Good afternoon, Mrs Schrag.

(HARRIET *eyes him coldly.*)

HARRIET: Sir.

CASSIDY: I've come to escort Andrew to the hearing....
To provide a bit of moral support.

HARRIET: Moral support? From you? The gallows have
been made because of you and now you want to take
him there?

CASSIDY: Perhaps you'd prefer if I wait outside?

HARRIET: I don't think you'd care to hear my
preferences concerning you.

CASSIDY: (*Excusing himself*) Mrs Schrag.

(CASSIDY *exits.* SCHRAG *enters.*)

HARRIET: Cassidy is waiting outside for you, along
with the jackals and hyenas.

SCHRAG: I wish you'd make an effort to forgive him.
He's trying to be a friend. He didn't know it would
come to this.

HARRIET: But you did. You were warned—by him,
by me.

SCHRAG: I didn't believe they'd go to this extreme.

HARRIET: You brought this on us yourself.

SCHRAG: Harriet, I need you on my side, not against me.

HARRIET: I went to visit Mrs Webster and the baby
this morning... *(Fighting tears)* She didn't invite me in....
She asked me not to call on her anymore.

SCHRAG: Good heavens, why?

HARRIET: *(Sudden vehemence)* Because of you, Andrew.
They think I'm the wife of a traitor. When they look
at me, I feel ashamed.

SCHRAG: Ashamed? You've done nothing wrong.

HARRIET: I told you this would happen. I told you.
Why couldn't you do what I begged of you and just
keep your head down?

SCHRAG: I only spoke the truth.

HARRIET: The truth is no defense against anything.

SCHRAG: This will pass. I'll be exonerated, you'll see...

HARRIET: That won't change anyone's mind. The
damage is done. People forget the good things,
they only remember the smear...

SCHRAG: I don't know what to do to help you.

He tries to take her in his arms, she pushes him away.

HARRIET: Bend, conciliate, give them what they want
for an hour or two, at least. Bow your stubborn head.

SCHRAG: What would people think of me if I did that?

HARRIET: They hate you now.

SCHRAG: But I don't yet hate myself.

HARRIET: Do you think this is still about your self-regard? Give them what they want. Please. Don't make it worse.

SCHRAG: Will you leave me no pride?

HARRIET: At what price? What is your pride worth to us? Until this is over, can't you hide your feelings?

SCHRAG: It's not my feelings, it's my principles.

HARRIET: Hide them, too.

SCHRAG: If you hide your principles, you don't have any.

HARRIET: Oh, for heaven's sake. Just do it.

SCHRAG: *(Angrily)* I can't. Don't you understand that? They've convicted a man for calling their regulations "a big joke". They're bringing charges against people because they don't buy liberty bonds. It's so blatantly wrong. ...Surely you can see some merit in opposing these people.

HARRIET: That's a very fine, noble posture. Now, for me, just for my ears, can we establish that you're doing this for your ego? That you want to show that you're smarter and better and more principled and made of finer stuff than he is? Just so we can talk about this to each other, will you admit that much?

SCHRAG: Of course I'm vain enough to think myself better than these venal, ignorant, cowardly, ambitious politicians who tell us to toss away our young men like tainted meat! Who doesn't think himself better? Do you think I'm not human?

HARRIET: There's no need to convince a wife that her husband is human.

SCHRAG: You make too much of it. I'm head of the German department, they won't fire me. This is all for show.

HARRIET: How can you be so intelligent and yet so stupid?

SCHRAG: *(Offended)* Stupid, is it?

HARRIET: I'm sorry, I didn't mean that...but you are.

SCHRAG: I see.

HARRIET: Stupid and proud and self-destructive, and yes, noble and honorable and brilliant, in your own way, and courageous—and stupid!

SCHRAG: Well, we've established that.

HARRIET: Make peace with them, whatever it takes. Make this go away.

SCHRAG: Damn it, woman, must you make it harder?

(Pause)

HARRIET: Am I "woman" now?

SCHRAG: I apologize, but you are relentless, relentless. You will have your own way no matter what.

HARRIET: Because I'm afraid! The world has gone crazy. What will happen to us? ...Andrew, this terrifies me, don't you understand?

SCHRAG: It terrifies me, too.

HARRIET: *(Surprised)* You don't mean that.

SCHRAG: I'm more frightened than you are. I know what they can do.

HARRIET: Don't say that; don't you say that. You're not supposed to be afraid. I count on you.

SCHRAG: I'm afraid to open my mouth about anything lest someone misconstrue it now. If they dug up slanders about Cassidy to make him cooperate, what will prevent them from doing even worse to me?

HARRIET: *(Dismissively)* What could they find about you?

SCHRAG: I've lived a life, Harriet, I'm no better than other men.

Everyone has reason to be fearful of that kind of scrutiny. It will take all the courage I have not to go into that hearing on my knees. I need your help, Harriet, even to pretend to courage.

HARRIET: Oh, Andrew—I've never seen you like this.

SCHRAG: You haven't known me long enough.

HARRIET: Why didn't you tell me you were afraid?

SCHRAG: If I hear myself whimpering, where do I look for courage? ...I have to fight, don't I? You tell me not to do it, but don't I have to? Am I not right in at least some small measure?

HARRIET: I can't call it right to stand in the path of a runaway horse.... What's the most important thing in your life? It's being head of the department, isn't it? You're so proud of being an educator.

SCHRAG: Well, I suppose...

HARRIET: If they find you guilty of sedition who would ever hire you to teach after that? You'll lose your position, you'll lose your place in the community.... You'll lose everything. Is it worth all that? You'll be left with nothing and no one but me. Is that enough, am I enough for you?

SCHRAG: That is an unfair question....

HARRIET: Because if I am, then why won't you do this one thing for me? And if I'm not...then why should I allow you to do this to us?

SCHRAG: *(Defeated)* I can't fight you and them.

HARRIET: If I were with child, would it matter? Would it change what you say at the hearing?

SCHRAG: Oh, my dear! Are you...?

HARRIET: I'm young, Andrew. I will have children. Would it matter? Would you have your child grow up with your shame?

SCHRAG: *(Resigned)* What would you have me do?

HARRIET: Whatever they ask of you.

SCHRAG: ...Yes, all right.

HARRIET: Whatever they need.

SCHRAG: Yes, all right.

Cassidy enters.

CASSIDY: Sorry to intrude, but it's getting late. I thought to go with you, Andrew, if you'll have me.

SCHRAG: Of course...Harriet...I'll do as you say.... But we must discuss the other matter.

HARRIET: I'll get my coat.

(Lights down on SCHRAG *home.)*

(Lights up on CHANCELLOR's *office.)*

Scene Nine

(CHANCELLOR's *office*)

(CHANCELLOR *is present as* SCHRAG *enters.*)

CHANCELLOR: Ah, Professor Schrag. I thought a word or two before we go into the hearing...

SCHRAG: Of course, Chancellor.

CHANCELLOR: I've spent a deal of time conferring with Mister Megrim. He is not an unreasonable man. A bit avid in his labors, to be sure, but he has quotas, he has to justify himself to his superiors.... You can see his position.

SCHRAG: I see mine a bit more sympathetically.

CHANCELLOR: We all have our point of view here, but I think that one factor we have in common is the desire not to harm the university.

SCHRAG: The university?

CHANCELLOR: I hardly need point out that it would be a terrible black mark on this institution if a prominent member of the faculty, the head of a department... um, uh, well, you see how it is.

SCHRAG: It will hardly benefit me, either.

CHANCELLOR: Naturally, I hate to see you in this trouble. I take you for a good and decent man, always have. I'm sure you meant no harm by your remarks.

SCHRAG: I didn't consider them harmful...

CHANCELLOR: There you are.

SCHRAG: ...merely truthful.

CHANCELLOR: Kindly don't joust with me. I don't pretend to have a large political perspective. But I know this: if you are found guilty, it will be assumed that there are others like you here. A university is famous for people with opinions. This is not the time for opinions.

SCHRAG: But, surely, freedom of speech and academic liberty affect the university most profoundly.

CHANCELLOR: That's very grand, but I hardly think that you, personally, carry the mantle of intellectual freedom on your shoulders, do you? Not when the opinion of the people is arrayed against you.

SCHRAG: This is not a war in the people's interest.
Wall Street has too much invested in British bonds
to risk a defeat. This is a war for commercial interests.
You know it and I know it.

CHANCELLOR: This hearing is not about what you and
I know, man! It's about power.
   If we don't exercise discretion, we will surely lose
what little we have.... Are you so arrogant that you
hold yourself above the institution that employs you?

SCHRAG: I want to cooperate with you, Chancellor.
What must I do?

CHANCELLOR: When you are asked if you support the
war, say yes. When you are asked if you support the
President, say yes. They'll consider it a victory; they
won't pursue the matter further. Just say yes and
then keep your opinions to yourself. Make no more
comments about the war, about politics, about anything
outside of your purview. Do this for the university,
Professor Schrag, and the university will be grateful
to you.

SCHRAG: *(Pause)* And that will mollify Megrim?

CHANCELLOR: I do not answer to Mister Megrim. I am
responsible to the Board of Regents of this university,
not to the Defense Council. This is my hearing, not
Megrim's. It will have the outcome I decide, but I will
not be embarrassed. Do not make me reveal my hand.
I will give you both some scope, but do not test my
patience.

SCHRAG: Will you allow me to speak?

CHANCELLOR: Within reason, but what do you gain by
braying your opinions to the world?

SCHRAG: My self-respect?

CHANCELLOR: You people in the humanities, what agonies you put yourselves through. Fortunately, chemistry is not a field that calls for an agonized soul. Let us cleave to the facts and we can't go far wrong. The fact is, I ask you for a few minutes of humility in exchange for um, uh...

SCHRAG: *(Pause)* I'm only one voice. There are others that are not silenced.

CHANCELLOR: Yes, well, one at a time, I suppose. Will you cooperate?

SCHRAG: I will bend as low as I can. My bones aren't used to it.

CHANCELLOR: You call that cooperation? You bristle with arrogance! Do not goad Megrim. He is highly motivated and not as simple as he seems—frankly, I think he despises education; or, the educated.

SCHRAG: I apologize. I don't wish to goad anyone. I will do all I can to cooperate.

CHANCELLOR: The university is grateful. Naturally, I, too, am uh, um...

SCHRAG: Thank you.

CHANCELLOR: Give me a few minutes with Megrim. We will await you upstairs when you're ready.

(SCHRAG exits.)

(Pause. MEGRIM enters.)

Scene Ten

(CHANCELLOR, MEGRIM)

CHANCELLOR: He's a good man, Schrag.

MEGRIM: You don't say.

CHANCELLOR: Oh, an excellent man. Intelligent, accomplished, full of integrity.

MEGRIM: And pride?

CHANCELLOR: He is a proud man, yes.

MEGRIM: Pride will pull him down like a chain around his neck.

CHANCELLOR: I'd rather he weren't pulled down.

MEGRIM: Some men don't want to be saved.

CHANCELLOR: He's highly respected. This is not a man to make a martyr of; he's too well regarded, too well known.

MEGRIM: Martyrs aren't made from whole cloth, it's a great vanity that demands that sort of recognition. They insist upon it. It's not the meek who volunteer for the stake and the fire, Chancellor, it's the haughty. I will offer him martyrdom. I will put it before him on a plate. I will bait him, bait him, bait him. If he's tempted, he's mine.

CHANCELLOR: I don't want him to be tempted. He's willing to compromise, he's highly reasonable.

MEGRIM: And highly disloyal.

CHANCELLOR: I don't believe his hubris extends to that.

MEGRIM: His what?

CHANCELLOR: Hubris... Well, it means exaggerated self-confidence.

MEGRIM: I know what it means. The question is, do you know what sedition means?

CHANCELLOR: Well, yes, I, uh, um...

MEGRIM: Because I know what it means. I know how it sounds, I know how it looks, I know how it tastes and smells. Don't you tell me whether or not a man is seditious, Chancellor. I make that judgment, and there won't be any confusion about my vocabulary, either.

CHANCELLOR: Well, not to be contentious, Mister Megrim, but I will be in charge of this hearing. I will make the judgment.

MEGRIM: And then I will make my judgment on the University.

CHANCELLOR: ...Are you suggesting the entire institution can be considered seditious?

MEGRIM: Why not?

CHANCELLOR: *(Angrily)* I assure you this university, and its board of regents, is the most loyal of institutions, as you will see in due course. We are prepared to make a considerable sacrifice to demonstrate that point. And I do not appreciate any suggestions to the contrary.

MEGRIM: *(Falsely meek)* I'm certain you know best, Chancellor. You are, after all, the Chancellor.

CHANCELLOR: Well...as you say...

MEGRIM: You must forgive my enthusiasm. I merely want to do my duty to this nation.

CHANCELLOR: I'm sure you love your country.

MEGRIM: Every boob loves his country just as every child loves his mother's breast. I appreciate this country, Chancellor. It's a nation of laws, not royal whims. Conform to the laws in America and you're safe. I burn with devotion to those laws and it frightens those who are less committed.

CHANCELLOR: Yes, well, let's try to control the conflagration, shall we?

MEGRIM: Conflagration? ...Oh, you mean fire. I do have to struggle to keep up with you people. *(He exits.)*

(Lights down on CHANCELLOR's *office.)*

(Lights up on the hearing room.)

Scene Eleven

(The Hearing Room)

(The "room" can take as much or as little of the stage as required.)

(CHANCELLOR sits as a presiding officer. MEGRIM paces as the interrogator. CASSIDY is in the background, one of the "audience" who witness the proceedings. SCHRAG enters and stands next to his seat.)

MEGRIM: Professor Schrag, it's so good to meet you at last. Everyone has so much to say about you.

SCHRAG: Indeed.

MEGRIM: You're not one of those folks who are difficult to see against the background. I call them the hazy people; no one knows where they stand. You are an oak among the saplings, it seems.... Of course it's the tallest tree that will be struck by lightning.

SCHRAG: By that reasoning, all trees would soon be the same height.... I realize you were speaking metaphorically, I was just being logical.

MEGRIM: Thank you for the instruction. I can see that I have much to learn in these hallowed halls. I shall have to be very careful in my choice of words. I'm just one of those hazy people, myself, I fear.

SCHRAG: I think your presence has been adequately noted here.

MEGRIM: Oh, not me. It's the office. Not the man but the uniform, as they say.

SCHRAG: And what uniform are you wearing, exactly?

MEGRIM: I represent the people of the United States and their patriotic desire for unity and security...

SCHRAG: Ah, patriotism. I thought I detected something.

MEGRIM: No need for detection with me, Professor. I am an unabashed patriot. I love my country.

SCHRAG: As do I, although I don't love all of the things it does.

MEGRIM: No nation is perfect, I'm sure, but this is not the time to find fault and criticize. We must all pull the rope together now. The nation requires enthusiasm for our task. That is why dissent is such a problem.

SCHRAG: Ministers are crying from the pulpit for German blood, both here and abroad. That's enthusiastic.

MEGRIM: Would you censor our men of faith? Freedom of religious belief is a precious right. We must be respectful of a man's religion.

SCHRAG: We must be respectful of a man's right to his religion; we are not required to be respectful of the belief itself. The Constitution does not ask us to respect every shade of nonsense just because it invokes the supernatural.

CHANCELLOR: The peculiarities of religion are beyond our scope in this hearing, thank God. If we could just, ah, um...

MEGRIM: Are you equally disdainful of every opinion you disagree with?

SCHRAG: Every man is free to voice his view on any folly—just as I am free to dispute it. It's called freedom of speech. I hold it precious.

MEGRIM: I couldn't agree more. Nothing is more precious than the freedom of speech—except the freedom of this country. We are here today because

of the possibility of sedition. And what is that but the
misuse of freedom of speech? Professor, what if you
whisper that so-and-so cheats on his exams? What is his
recourse against such a rumor? Shouldn't you be held
responsible for this slander? Well, a private citizen can
confront you or he can sue you. But what if you defame
the government? ...This is a simple business. Some
people are saying things that are counter to the
war effort. Now, the war effort isn't just one man's
opinion—that's what freedom of speech is all about,
every man has a right to his opinion—but war isn't
one man's opinion. War is a national commitment,
war requires unity and sacrifice from all of us. Other
men might go to war for their king or their emperor,
but the United States can't ask you to do that, there
is no king. We are a democracy; we go to war for the
people, for each other. Only congress can declare war
and congress represents all of us, all of us.

If the United States commits itself to war it's because
all of us have jointly said, "Yes, regrettable though it is,
the reasons compel us to join hands and fight for one
another, for our mutual good, for our mutual safety".
That is how things are in a democracy. When a vote
is taken and a winner determined, we don't continue
to electioneer against him, we don't deny his right to
govern, we accept the election, the will of the people
prevails. There is great wisdom in that. This country is
based on belief in the wisdom of the people. The time
for debate is before actions are taken, not after. What
shall happen if those who criticize our participation
in this war are allowed to rant in bitterness because
they're too fearful?

A man at war does not need someone tugging at him,
urging him to go home. What would happen if the
protestors prevailed? Why, some men would cease to
fight, the group would be weakened, the group would
lose, the war would be lost. The brave men who died

would have died in vain. Can this country—can any country—allow this to happen? Of course not... There is a time for freedom of speech—no one is more in favor of that freedom than I—but there is also a time, recognized by all wise men, when the freedom to remain silent is more important.... And so, certain types of speech are not permitted, and rightly so. Those of us safe at home are no less at war than the men fighting for us in the trenches. The effect of that cowardly urging is no less dangerous here than in France. It puts us all in peril.

SCHRAG: I don't believe a war has ever been lost because of freedom of speech. I do know that freedom of speech has been lost because of a war. No war lasts forever, but the freedom may be gone irretrievably.

MEGRIM: If we lose this war, all freedoms will be lost.

SCHRAG: How are we to lose this war? You speak of our defense...

CHANCELLOR: Professor, I don't think...

MEGRIM: Quite all right.

CHANCELLOR: There's really no need to respond...

MEGRIM: I welcome his opinion. We don't want to stifle him. I urge you to speak freely, Professor.

SCHRAG: It's only a question. Germany has no navy on the high seas. They can't get out of port because of mines and the British blockade. Is it possible they are going to transport an army of half a million men to America in submarines? Their manpower is depleted, they are conscripting teenagers and old men, we are separated by an ocean. What threat do they offer us? They cannot attack us, they cannot invade us, they are weak and spent and locked in a death spiral with Britain and France. It is not always clear what

Americans have to fear from them. I ask you again, what threat has compelled us to go to war?

MEGRIM: One threat is the attack on our minds, Professor. I don't need to tell you the power of ideology.

SCHRAG: Our government is already "defending" our minds with the Committee on Public Information. They're encouraging children to keep watch on their parents and neighbor to observe neighbor, lest any wrong thinking slip in. Some states have outlawed music by Beethoven, that famous enemy. We are told we can't speak German on the telephone because the operator can't listen in if we do.

MEGRIM: Why would you want to speak German? This is America.

SCHRAG: Twenty percent of our population is of German descent and they're loyal Americans, whatever language they speak.

MEGRIM: Most of them are loyal, but it's everyone's job to find those who aren't. You're German yourself, aren't you, Professor?

SCHRAG: I'm a German-American.

MEGRIM: What's that? Half-cat, half-dog? You can't have it both ways. You speak German, you teach German, you even spend summers in Berlin, don't you?

SCHRAG: In the past. I received grants to study. I haven't gone since the war began for fear that my ship would be sunk, illegally, by the British, even though the U S was neutral.

MEGRIM: (To CHANCELLOR) You give grants to study in Germany?

CHANCELLOR: The grants are from the University of Berlin, let me make that clear.

MEGRIM: Oh, very nice. They must think very highly of you in Berlin. Do you perform some service for them, perhaps?

SCHRAG: I study.

MEGRIM: But you're already a professor.

SCHRAG: Education doesn't stop because you have credentials. It's a life-long endeavor.

MEGRIM: What do you find so admirable amongst the cabbage-eaters?

SCHRAG: Their literature, their music, their science, their system of education, their manners...

MEGRIM: Yes, yes, yes...America is such an uncultured place, isn't it? We hear that all the time—Europe looking down its long nose at us. It must be difficult for a man like you to put up with all of the hoi polloi here in this country. I'm surprised you don't live there.

SCHRAG: My parents made the choice to leave there and live here. I see no reason to reverse their decision.

MEGRIM: Now there's a lukewarm endorsement of America.
   Germany is the land of your heritage, your parents, your language, your preferences... You're a German at heart yourself, aren't you?

SCHRAG: No.

MEGRIM: Are you ashamed to be German?

SCHRAG: Of course not.

MEGRIM: Then why not admit it? It's only natural that you would love Germany. You would hate to see your fellow Germans in trouble, their culture sullied, all these insults here in America; it's only natural that you'd support Germany in the war.

SCHRAG: I do not support Germany in the war.

MEGRIM: Really? Does that mean you support America?

SCHRAG: ...I don't wish us to lose.

MEGRIM: Paring that cheese pretty fine, aren't you? Not "wishing us to lose" is not the same as supporting us.

SCHRAG: My position is nuanced, Mister Megrim.

MEGRIM: Nuanced? Isn't that just another word for slippery? I say a thing is or it isn't. Are you a true American or not?

SCHRAG: True?

CHANCELLOR: What is the point of all this, Mister Megrim?

MEGRIM: Just trying to establish who he is. Seems to be rather difficult.

CHANCELLOR: Professor Schrag, are you an American citizen?

SCHRAG: Of course.

CHANCELLOR: *(To* MEGRIM*)* There you are. Not so hard, after all. Now, gentlemen, I see no reason to drag the matter on any longer than necessary. Do let's try to deal with this matter in fewer words. No speeches, no speeches. I'm sure we all regret certain excesses of patriotism that have occurred domestically, while applauding the virtues of necessary patriotism in the cause of um, uh...but this hearing is not about the freedom of speech or loyalties of the heart or anything else. It's a question of whether Professor Schrag has committed sedition. The point is, Professor, you have said and written some things that might be interpreted as obstructionist—uh—vis-a-vis the war. Not your intention, I'm sure.

MEGRIM: That's what we're here to determine.

(HARRIET *enters silently and joins* CASSIDY *in the background.*)

CHANCELLOR: Indeed. So, if we could proceed systematically, let's go through the list provided by the act of Congress as it defines sedition. Professor, was it ever your intention to... *(Reading)* "abuse the flag of the United States"?

SCHRAG: No, though many have. Since the charges of this hearing were announced, I was approached by a mob demanding that I kiss the flag as proof of my loyalty.

MEGRIM: And did you?

SCHRAG: I did not. I won't treat the flag of my country as if it were the Pope's ring.

MEGRIM: Nor give proof of your loyalty?

SCHRAG: I could wrap myself in it like a winding sheet and it wouldn't prove anything. Hypocrisy is not revealed by the touch of cloth.

CHANCELLOR: Were these hooligans students?

SCHRAG: Not mine, but they were students. Mine would not treat me that way, I think.

MEGRIM: Let's speak of your students, then. Did you ever tell a student of this university not to enlist in the army?

SCHRAG: I'm not sure what you refer to.

MEGRIM: Oh, I'm sorry. Was I difficult to understand? I must try harder to make myself clear.
   I'm talking about a conversation that you had with a student at this university in which you advised him not to enlist in the army... Did you discuss the firepower of the German machine gun? Casualty figures? Shipping losses? ...Did you tell this boy that democracy wasn't worth defending?

SCHRAG: You refer to Herman Tellig.

MEGRIM: How shall I record that response? Yes? No?

CHANCELLOR: Did you have such a conversation, Professor?

MEGRIM: Let me help you. This would have been April 4th.

SCHRAG: I remember the spirit of the conversation, not the details.

MEGRIM: Oh, come along, Professor. Your memory is better than that. I'm told you can quote reams of German poetry—in German. Surely you can remember a conversation in which you told one of your students not to defend our country.

CHANCELLOR: Did you say April 4th? We were not at war until April 6th, Mr. Megrim. This conversation, whatever it was, is not germane if we weren't yet at war. We have all said things at various times that, uh, um...it's not relevant.

MEGRIM: How would you counsel a student today, Professor? Have you changed your mind?

CHANCELLOR: I'm no lawyer, but that does seem to be asking for speculation, Mr. Megrim. Let's move on. Now, Professor Schrag, since the United States has been at war, again, since the war began, have you *(Reads)* "being physically able to work, remained idle when useful employment is obtainable"...I think we can skip that one?

(MEGRIM *dismissively waves* CHANCELLOR *on.*)

CHANCELLOR: "Utter, print, write, or publish anything disloyal, profane, scurrilous, or abusive about the uniform of the Army or Navy...?"

SCHRAG: The uniform?

CHANCELLOR: Yes, well, fashion is not our real concern here. Did you "wilfully utter, print, write, or publish any disloyal, profane, scurrilous, or abusive language about the form of government of the United States"?

SCHRAG: The form of government? We are a republic. I have no quarrel with that.

MEGRIM: Our democracy, Professor. Our way of life.

SCHRAG: It isn't our way of life, it isn't even the way we administer our political system, we just pretend that it is.

MEGRIM: It isn't? That's interesting. I'm so glad we're having this conversation.

SCHRAG: What do you think democracy means, Mister Megrim?

MEGRIM: I'm not one of your students, Professor. I don't have to answer—especially since I'm sure you have a better answer. But I'd say rule by the people.

SCHRAG: We like to think of it that way, don't we? All of the people casting their free and independent ballot. But half of the country are women, and they can't vote. Most of the colored citizens in the southern states are excluded by property requirements, literacy tests, and simple intimidation. What's that, another ten percent? This is a nation of an unending flow of immigrants; they can't vote. Another ten percent? How many free and independent voters does that leave us? Thirty percent? But, sadly, how many of them can be troubled to vote? Two thirds? Not that many, but let's say so. That leaves twenty percent, Mister Megrim. And how many of those owe a greater allegiance to their church to secure their salvation or to the political machines, the Tammany Halls that buy their votes for a beer and a free lunch, or the employers who threaten to fire them? ...How many cast their ballots automatically for

their party affiliation unwittingly, as though they
were supporting a sporting team? What have we left?
Ten percent who cast a free and independent ballot?
And our candidates are elected with a mere majority
of that—or, in President Wilson's case, less than fifty
percent of the vote the first time...This is democracy
as it is practiced in this country, Mister Megrim.
I don't think I have defamed it by defining it, have I?

CHANCELLOR: Shorter answers, please. Shorter, shorter.

MEGRIM: Chancellor, could we stop dancing around
the subject? We're not here for a lesson in political
philosophy. We're here because of the war. We're here
because this man opposes the war and all that it stands
for.

SCHRAG: I'm not sure what it stands for.

MEGRIM: You know what I mean. For all your shilly-
shallying and mincing words and splitting hairs,
you know what I mean. Are you afraid to speak about
the war?

SCHRAG: You want my thoughts about the war?

MEGRIM: I do.

CHANCELLOR: Let's keep this relevant, shall we? Did
you "abuse or defame the military forces of the United
States"?

SCHRAG: I wouldn't defame the military forces, I mourn
for them. There will be hundreds, perhaps thousands,
of young men from this institution alone who will live
in unspeakable filth and squalor in trenches roiling
with rats and lice and corpses of both sides walled into
the mud and pressed into the earth underfoot...they are
dying already. Young men I have taught, young men
I have known, and you, Chancellor.
    Young men who have been our responsibility will die
in France and Belgium with their throats burning, with

their lungs filling with mucus, gasping for breath,
blinded by a gas that attacks not only the lungs,
but the armpits, the eyes, the scrotum...

CHANCELLOR: It is not the weapons of war that are at
issue here! Shall our armies lack something the enemy
has? Confine your remarks, Professor. Confine them.

MEGRIM: There are women present, man.

SCHRAG: The women will suffer greatly, too, from
the loss of their sons and their husbands and their
brothers.... That's what I have written and said about
the men in our military. Does this defame them?
Unless you believe that there will be no casualties
in the war because America has entered it, no one is
defamed by saying that many, many are doomed to die.

MEGRIM: War is famous for causing death, Professor.
That does not mean we must be afraid to fight.

SCHRAG: We must be afraid to fight unnecessarily.

MEGRIM: Unnecessarily? The President of the United
States says it's necessary. The Congress of the United
States says it's necessary. Do you know more than the
Congress?

SCHRAG: Congress is nothing more than a bag full of
Congressmen. Have you ever met one who didn't make
you want to wash your hands?
   Do you really need Congress to tell you what to think,
Mister Megrim?

MEGRIM: What office have you been elected to,
Professor? How have the people displayed their trust
in your judgment? The people of this country are not
afraid of a scrap, nor is our President, if the cause is
right.

SCHRAG: I know. Since he's been elected, Wilson
has sent troops into Haiti, the Dominican Republic,

Nicaragua, and Mexico, and now Europe. He seems able to find a cause to fight just about anywhere he looks.

CHANCELLOR: Let's limit our focus. You have not defamed our military. Excellent. Now, you certainly have not *(Reads)* "urged, incited, or advocated any curtailment of the production, in this country, of any thing necessary or essential to the conduct of the war," have you?

SCHRAG: Only war lovers and profiteers.

CHANCELLOR: Schrag, you're trying my patience. This phrase clearly refers to goods and materials and you haven't advocated any curtailment of production in this country, per se, have you?

SCHRAG: No. Not per se.

CHANCELLOR: Excellent. Per se is what we're after. Well, there we are, then. Thank you, Professor. Mister Megrim, I think that concludes the matter...

MEGRIM: We're not finished!

CHANCELLOR: Personally, Mister Megrim, I've heard enough.

MEGRIM: I haven't. The people of this country haven't. We won't be satisfied with this white-wash. Professor Schrag, once and for all, do you support the war or don't you?

SCHRAG: *(Pause)* That's a complicated question.

MEGRIM: Those of us not teaching in a university don't have the luxury of thinking complicated thoughts. If we have an enemy, we don't dither, we don't get lost in details, we fight him until he is defeated.... Come, Professor, give us an answer.

SCHRAG: I have given you much already. You have taken my good name by bringing me to this ludicrous "hearing" in which no one wants to hear what I have to say.

MEGRIM: I want to hear. I urge you to speak. No more circumlocutions—did I use that word correctly? Oh, good... Do you support this war or don't you?

CHANCELLOR: It seems to me...

MEGRIM: I will hear his answer! Come, Professor, you're an honest man, are you not? You'll tell us the truth once you get finished with your nuances and your fish-tailing and your evasions.

You're a proud man; you have pride in what you believe. Or do you now think you were in error?

SCHRAG: In error?

MEGRIM: Isn't it possible, Professor, that, despite your learning and your position, you were just plain wrong and the President was right about this war?

SCHRAG: *(pause)* Do you refer to the war for liberty that we're engaged in right now?

MEGRIM: Of course.

SCHRAG: Everyone in the country is battling for liberty, Mister Megrim, whether they know it or not, but it's not an external enemy that can take away our liberty; we are always perilously close to doing it to ourselves... because it's so easy to give up. Freedom is heavy, freedom is hard, freedom is a burden. It would be such a relief to surrender it to all the tyrants, the Church, the state, all the powerful men that would relieve us of the nuisance and frustration of listening to other people speak their minds. The men who wrote our constitution cried out for all the world to hear the incredible statement that we, the people, the common people of the United States of America, had freedoms. Freedom to speak, freedom to assemble, freedom to worship. There has never been a document like it.

All the tablets of scripture, every boss and bully in history, every priest and politician tells us what we shall not do; only our Bill of Rights tells us what we are free to do...It happened only once, and, if it's gone, it may not be renewable because it is assaulted constantly, fervently, by those with power who know it is all that stands between them and complete control. Tell a European serf or peasant what to do and he will do it. He is untroubled by notions of his right to defy his superiors or his right to have his own opinion about what is to be done—because he has no such right. But tell an American what to do and there is something in his character of the teenaged boy rounding to maturity, a stiff-necked insistence that age and position do not confer wisdom, that his life is his own and he will live it as he will. Why does an American of forty or fifty years still feel this way? Because he knows he has the freedom to do so, that it is enshrined in his Constitution, that it, truly, is the lasting will of his people—the one beacon that persists despite the excitements of the moment, the hysteria, the deceits, the efforts of those meaning well and ill alike to change it, the inadequacies of our voting, the shifting winds of world events... Despite all those, there remains that proud, insistent voice within every American that says, "I am free, I am free." The struggle to remain free is the war that all of us are engaged in every day. I support that war, Mister Megrim. I support that never-ending war.

(CASSIDY *rises and applauds, loudly.*)

CASSIDY: Bravo! Bravo!

CHANCELLOR: That will do. Is there anyone present who would speak against Professor Schrag? *(Hastily)* Clearly not.

MEGRIM: Chancellor, I protest...

CHANCELLOR: *(Continuing quickly)* I find a complete absence of evidence against Professor Schrag and his standing is declared to be as good as though no accusation had been brought...

MEGRIM: His every breath is arrogant defiance!

CHANCELLOR: I heard no proof of sedition.

MEGRIM: How could you not?

CHANCELLOR: ...I declare this hearing over.

MEGRIM: This is a conspiracy.

CHANCELLOR: It is done, Mister Megrim.

MEGRIM: You can not declare this man innocent...

CHANCELLOR: I have done so! It is over, Mister Megrim! Over!

MEGRIM: It is *not. (He exits.)*

(HARRIET *rushes to* SCHRAG. CASSIDY *crosses hurriedly after her.)*

HARRIET: Andrew, I didn't understand that it was so important. I'm so proud of you.

(CASSIDY *joins them.)*

CASSIDY: Congratulations, Andrew!

SCHRAG: Thank you, my friend. And thank you for your support.

CASSIDY: What a victory! Wasn't he glorious, Harriet?

HARRIET: I've never been so proud.

CASSIDY: I knew it would all work out well. We must celebrate!

(CHANCELLOR *approaches them.)*

CHANCELLOR: Professor Schrag, a word.

SCHRAG: Of course... *(To others)* I'll join you soon.
We'll celebrate.

(HARRIET *and* CASSIDY *move away and exit.)*

SCHRAG: Thank you for your assistance, Chancellor.

CHANCELLOR: What did you imagine you were doing?
You were insolent and provocative and clearly in
violation of our agreement. We had an agreement,
sir, we had an agreement.

SCHRAG: I said nothing that I didn't believe.

CHANCELLOR: Good god, man, who cares what you
believe? Do you think you impeded the war machine
by so much as a second? The dogs are loosed and they
must be fed. Do you have a son or brother who will
have to go?

SCHRAG: No.

CHANCELLOR: Then why risk yourself like that?

SCHRAG: I want people to learn. I'm a teacher.

CHANCELLOR: That's only a profession, not a reason
for suicide.

SCHRAG: If it's only a profession, then one is not a
teacher.

CHANCELLOR: Spare me all of that high-sounding
tosh...Why goad these people? It might inspire an
underclassman, but it's like a red flag to someone
like Megrim.... He's terrified because you threaten his
mindless adherence to the rules. He thinks those rules
are the belt that holds the universe together. But you,
you're dangerous, you're chaos and ruin. What would
happen if everyone went around practicing his
"freedoms"? The average man doesn't know what his
freedoms are and doesn't exercise them. He worships
the gods his parents gave him and agrees with the
loudest voice he hears, he does what he's told and he's

happy to do so—it relieves him of the burden of thinking. If everyone said and acted as he wished, authority would be forced to sit upon us like a stone on an egg. We have freedom only as long as we don't exercise it.

SCHRAG: The Constitution says...

CHANCELLOR: The Constitution is a document, it's not a way of life. The "freedoms" you're talking about were a negotiation between a handful of wealthy, educated, powerful men who didn't trust each other for a second. They were protecting themselves, not the people.

SCHRAG: That is very cynical.

CHANCELLOR: You didn't just offer yourself as a martyr with your inflammatory remarks. You exposed me, too, because I had no choice but to save you from yourself. Well, at least you'll do no further harm at this institution.

SCHRAG: What do you mean?

CHANCELLOR: I mean you are no longer a member of this institution.

SCHRAG: Do you mean that I'm fired?

CHANCELLOR: Fired? How could I fire you after I've just declared you without blame? ...But we no longer have a position for you here. The Regents have decided to abolish the German department.

SCHRAG: Abolish the department? How can you do that?

CHANCELLOR: I didn't do it, the Regents did it. They, too, are wealthy, educated, powerful men. Whom did you think they would side with?

We shall treat the German language and its literature and its culture as if it had never existed. As Megrim would say, it's what the people want.

SCHRAG: You can't do that, it's unthinkable. The science, the medicine, the culture...

CHANCELLOR: It is done. We shall not teach it, we shall not study it, we shall not acknowledge it.

SCHRAG: You knew this before the hearing.

CHANCELLOR: Of course.

SCHRAG: Then why did you defend me?

CHANCELLOR: We couldn't have a head of department defamed. How would that look? It would be an embarrassment to me and to the Regents. Good day to you, Schrag. I hope you find comfort in your "truth."

(CHANCELLOR *exits.* SCHRAG *is alone onstage, stricken. Enter* HARRIET, *slowly.*)

HARRIET: I heard him.

SCHRAG: ...I only asked them to think. What did I do so terribly wrong?

HARRIET: You asked them to think.... Was it worth it?

SCHRAG: Harriet, I'm so sorry....

(HARRIET *puts up her hand to stop* SCHRAG.)

HARRIET: Was it worth it?

SCHRAG: *(Pause)* I can live with myself, at least.

HARRIET: Yes, but you have to live with me.... Come, Andrew, I'll take you home.

(Curtain)

END OF PLAY